Cocktails for Wimps

Cocktails for Wimps

Salvatore Calabrese

Photography by James Duncan

Sterling Publishing Co., Inc.
New York

Created by Lynn Bryan, The BookMaker, London
Design by Mary Staples
Photography by James Duncan
Editor: Beverly LeBlanc

Library of Congress Cataloging-in-Publication
Data Available

Published by Sterling Publishing Company, Inc.
387 Park Avenue South,
New York, NY 10016

© 2002 by Salvatore Calabrese

Printed in China
All rights reserved

Sterling ISBN 0-8069-8509-7

Distributed in Canada by
Sterling Publishing
c/o Canadian Manda Group,
One Atlantic Avenue, Suite 105,
Toronto, Ontario, Canada M6K 3EZ

Distributed in Great Britain and Europe by
Cassell PLC
Wellington House, 125 Strand,
London WC2R OBB, England

Distributed in Australia by
Capricorn Link (Australia) Pty Ltd.,
P.O. Box 704, Windsor,
NSW 2756 Australia

To Sue, with love and thanks

Contents

When I was asked to write this book, I was surprised to hear the words **wimps** and *cocktails* used together in a sentence. I don't know this word "wimps." *I am Italian and in my country, there are no wimps. Really.* We might ride small, zippy motor scooters and not thundering Harley Davidsons, but we are not wimps. The same tenet applies to cocktails. Cocktails are *cool*, **exciting**, *delicious*, and **macho**—not wimpy in the least. They are colorful characters, capable of working on many levels to delight and amuse. The two words don't mix . . .

. . . So my friends explained to me that being a wimp is OK; not cool, but it's OK. It's not a bad thing. Besides, in this case, it's used affectionately. A wimp can be either sex, and is really in need of a friend to show him the way. Especially with the art of making cocktails.

As my colleagues pointed out, making a cocktail is as easy as one, two, three for me since I do it all day, every day. I have mixed spirits and cordials since I was 11 years old, working for the summer in a romantic hotel on Italy's Amalfi Coast. So for me, cocktails are imbued with a magical quality. For others, the idea of mixing Triple Sec ("What?" I hear you cry!) with brandy and a dash of anisette is a nerve-wracking experience to be avoided at all cost.

These Ws give up too easily, turning to the bottle of chilled white wine instead. They know how to draw a cork. No disaster area there. (Well, yes, the cork can disintegrate into the wine, but with modern corks being made of plastic, this is less likely to happen.) It's the same with a can of beer. Flick off the cap and pour into a glass—or not. Simple.

We are all acquainted with a wimp: He's the neighbor who asks you to a barbecue and serves up half-cooked food—he doesn't flame it in case he sets fire to something other than the spareribs. Or, the lottery player who doesn't play because he knows he won't win. Unfortunately, until this frailty is conquered, they will not be able to experience the *frisson* given by an exotic cocktail; the moment it is mixed, it comes alive. It presents two treats: color and taste, two of my talents.

In this book I hope to banish the wimp in you; to bring you to the point where words like "crushed ice" don't bring to mind penguins stomping on a thin ice shelf in the Arctic Ocean, but instead conjure images of romance and desire in a glass, crackling and enticing as ice-cold vodka or gin is poured into it. Add a touch of cranberry juice and watch the color seep down through the crushed ice. The result: A fabulously lip-smacking cocktail.

This book is for these Ws, men or women, who want to create exotic cocktails, but have not considered they can ever achieve this ambition. I am convinced that after trying a few of the easy-to-make drinks featured in this book, you will become an expert. The first section takes you through what you will need in the way of tools and equipment; essentials for a spirits store cupboard; the different types of ice; glassware—it doesn't matter if you have a bottle of vintage Pol Roger and not a crystal champagne glass in sight —that's fine. You can serve champagne in a jelly glass as long as you serve it with style. We've taken this concept a little further. If you don't have a martini glass, use a small wine glass. The drink will still taste the same.

Yet, that was not satisfactory to a young man I met in my local home-furnishing store. I was taking a break from writing recipes, including the Cosmopolitan. He was searching the shelves for cocktail glasses—and I happened to be there looking for an old-fashioned glass. The assistant, chic, yet fresh out of school, asked another what a cocktail glass looked like. I was so shocked that someone working in a glassware department didn't know that universal fact, I spoke up. "It looks like a triangle on a central stem. There are none in this section," I said to the harassed man. He looked even more anxious. "I need four by 5 p.m. because I have guests coming for cocktails." It was 4 p.m. As it happened, I had recently been given a set of cocktail glasses and I already had several. I decided at that moment to give the new set to him.

"I have a set of four if that helps. I live across the street so it won't take long to get them." The anxiety went from his face as he looked upon his savior (Salvatore, by the way, is Italian for savior). "Thank you," he said. Then, "You don't have a recipe for a Cosmopolitan, do you?"

After glassware comes a glossary of terms you might not be familiar with, such as muddling or pousse-café (no, it's not a chill-out zone for cats). And once you've journeyed through those pages, you will learn how to be organized on the day, plus some presentation skills. The drink can be superbly fragrant, but if it is not presented well... Often the garnish is the one attraction that tempts guests to be adventurous with their palate. We're not talking intricate rose petals sculpted out of

carrots, just interesting effects made with pineapple, cranberries, blueberries, the humble lemon and orange peel, kiwifruit (otherwise known as the Chinese gooseberry), and one of my favorites, the elegant, pale-skinned star fruit. Step-by-step photographs of how to make a garnish perch decadently on the glass's rim reveal how easy it is to impress your friends.

For me, one of the important sections is that dealing with flavor. The secret to a great cocktail, one that is remembered for decades, even immortalized, is to reach a harmony of flavors—the balance of sweet and sour on the palate. Too much citrus and the drink is acid; too much sweet and the drink becomes sickening to the taste. There are also spicy flavors to add, giving the cocktail a kick! Subtlety is the key, and in this section I will explain how to achieve the essential, delicate balance.

Then you will reach the recipes. Here, I begin by introducing you to the mixing glass, a bartender's essential tool. I also explain how to make a drink directly into a glass, known as building a drink.

We then move to creating cocktails where a fruit (or mint leaves) must be muddled, or mashed, before the spirit is added. Then we move to creating cocktails in the shaker, mixing the ingredients in a shower of ice. Once you've become competent at shaking it all about, it's onto more interesting drinks that require a little more skill. You have probably noticed layers of

liquid in some drinks and wondered, how do they do that? Drinks like the B-52 and the ubiquitous Irish Coffee are both layered. It's all to do with chemistry and being an alchemist: I will teach you the tricks.

Next comes a unique opportunity to create a cocktail for the one you admire. Or even love. Something delicious which reflects their unique personality. I have created many of these personality cocktails: For my wife, Sue, I devised Sweet Sue; for a guy named Mac who comes to the bar regularly, the Mac Martini was created, and Champagne Wonder is perfectly suited to the palate and character of the recording artist Stevie Wonder.

This is followed by a short chapter of three party punches. Finally, a collection of nonalcoholic recipes. Given the current trend for healthy living, here are a few colorful, textured cocktails that will tempt the taste buds and fool everyone into thinking you have an incredibly sexy drink in your hand.

The people you see photographed in this book are friends and acquaintances, chosen because they are interested in cocktails, yet have not previously been tempted to test their skills at making them. Their verdict at the end of the shoot? "Fantastic." Each gave a resounding endorsement to their newly acquired art. It's my sincere hope that you, too, will enjoy the step-by-step learning process enough to feel sufficiently confident to throw a successful cocktail party soon.

By now you want to stop reading and begin. Right? **Sit back,** *relax,* and *kick your shoes off.* Now is the time to build your confidence slowly but surely as we build cocktails ranging from a simple *Negroni* to a *Tequila Sunrise.* It's time for cocktails for wimps. . .

Enjoy!

The

Basics

Tools of the Mix Master

There are certain tools and equipment that can help you make delicious cocktails. Most are inexpensive and can be found in the kitchen/bar section of a supermarket or any department store. If you don't have some of the items here, and don't want to buy them, look for substitutes in your kitchen utensils drawer. As long as it can do the required task, it will be OK to use.

SHAKER
Used for mixing various spirits and juices together over ice.

JUICER
Important for making fresh orange, lemon, and lime juices.

ICE BUCKET AND TONGS
There's a choice of metal, silver, or glass designs. Make sure the bucket is wide enough to hold lots of ice.

a   COCKTAIL SHAKER
b   JUICER
c   ICE BUCKET AND TONGS
d   MORTAR AND PESTLE
e   HAMILTON BEACH BLENDER
f   MIXING GLASS
g   GLASS POURER

MORTAR AND PESTLE

Used for muddling fruits or any other ingredient that needs mashing, such as mint.

BLENDER

Bartenders are loyal to one brand: The Hamilton Beach blender. However, any brand will suffice! Essential for summer cocktails when combining liquor and fruit with ice.

h	SMALL GRATER
i	CHAMPAGNE STOPPER
j	STRAWBERRY HULLER
k	COCKTAIL STICKS
l	SALT AND PEPPER GRINDERS
m	PONY-JIGGER
n	MUDDLER
o	MEAT TENDERIZER
p	KITCHEN TOWEL
q	CHOPPING BOARD

MIXING GLASS

Used for mixing two or more spirits with a bar spoon. Usually made of glass. You can use a glass or small jug with a lip instead.

POURER

Used for drops and dashes of bitters and some colored liqueurs. It's easier to pour from this type of vessel than from a bottle: You can judge the amount better.

GRATER

Used when dusting a drink with chocolate or nutmeg.

CHAMPAGNE STOPPER

Useful for saving the bubbles in a champagne bottle.

STRAWBERRY HULLER

Used to take the stem and hull from a strawberry.

COCKTAIL STICKS

Small wooden sticks for spearing pieces of fruit and cherries for garnishes.

SALT AND PEPPER GRINDERS

Used in drinks such as the Bloody Mary.

PONY-JIGGER

Important for measuring to balance the flavor and strength of a cocktail.

MUDDLER

Used when you need to mash sprigs of mint or berries into a pulp, usually in the bottom of an old-fashioned glass.

MEAT TENDERIZER

Useful for smashing ice wrapped in a kitchen towel (see page 20).

CHOPPING BOARD

There is a choice of wood or plastic types.

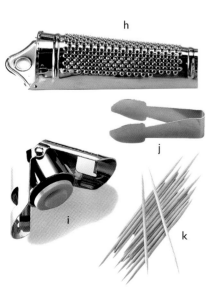

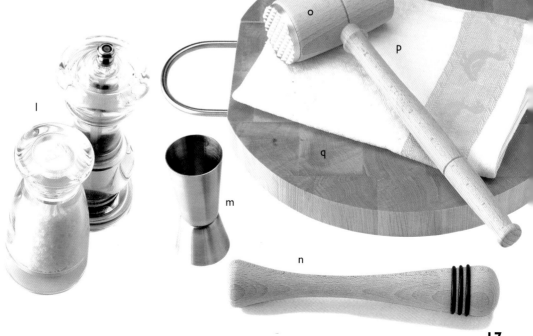

SPOON STRAINER

Useful to hold back ice and fruit when straining liquids.

ICE SCOOP

Essential. You can use a large ice-cream scoop or a clean plastic cup instead.

BAR SPOON

This has a small bowl at the end of a long handle. A long-handled dessert spoon is OK, too.

BAR KNIFE

A small, sharp knife used for slicing fruit.

CORKSCREW

Essential for opening wine bottles.

BOTTLE OPENER

These come in a variety of shapes and sizes. Choose the least-complicated opener that feels good in your hand, and is strong enough to last a few years.

a   SPOON STRAINER

b   ICE SCOOP

c   BAR SPOON

d   BAR KNIFE

e   CORKSCREW

f   BOTTLE OPENER

g   POURER

h   ZESTER

i   MELON BALLER

j   LONG STIRRERS

k   STRAWS

l   SHORT STIRRERS

m   COASTERS

n   GLASS PITCHER

POURER

One of these is useful for placing in the top of small glass containers or a bottle.

ZESTER

Used on lemon, orange, and lime peels to make garnishes.

MELON BALLER

Used for making small balls of soft fruit, such as melons, to use as a garnish.

STIRRERS

Stirrers are works of art—in glass or silver, with patterns and characters. Some Italian handblown glass stirrers are amusing, with tropical fish or berries designed as a grip. Plain glass or silver stirrers are also chic. Alternatively, use lacquered chopsticks or a spoon handle—but don't serve the cocktail with the latter!

STRAWS

Use large straws so the liquid can be easily sucked, especially when fruit juices or a heavier liquid is in the recipe. One straw is enough for a small glass; for goblets and summer-style drinks, use two.

DECORATIVE COASTERS

Use these if you have glass or precious tabletops that mark easily.

PITCHER FOR PUNCH

Glass displays the color of punches, especially when they are filled with floating slices of fruit and sprigs of mint. Or, you can use a large china soup tureen.

All About Ice

The most important thing about ice in a bar is: It must be fresh and dry.

Use the best filtered water to make ice and, if you prefer, use bottled

spring water. *Ice should taste only of water.*

Ice is used in a blender, a shaker, a mixing glass, or directly in a glass. Why do you need ice? Ice is used to insure the spirits are cooled as they are poured into a glass. Remember not to use the ice remaining in a shaker for the next drink because the ice will be broken and will retain the flavor of the previous drink.

Ice is available crushed, shaved, cracked, or cubed. The difference is that cracked and shaved ice are more watery than dry ice cubes. When added to a drink, the spirit is more immediately diluted. With solid ice cubes, the ice holds its water longer through the sipping. The ice melts ever more slowly.

The recipes in this book use only dry, hard ice cubes and crushed ice. As a general rule, ice cubes are used for cocktails made in a shaker. Crushed ice is used for drinks created in a blender.

Many top-quality refrigerators make both ice cubes and crushed ice. If you do not own one of these luxury items, crush your own using the method shown (right). Or buy a domestic ice-crusher from your local store. This is an added expense and only worthwhile if you intend to make a lot of cocktails over the coming years!

Some ice cube trays produce fun shapes such as stars, triangles, and hearts. These add an interesting visual touch in cocktails made for a special occasion.

CRUSHING ICE

The easiest way to make crushed ice is to smash ice cubes with a meat tenderizer. Wrap a handful of ice cubes in a kitchen towel. Hold the towel in one hand and smash the cubes with the meat tenderizer until the cubes are in small fragments.

Measuring & Terms

MEASURING

A double-ended pony-jigger is an important tool to use when making cocktails because it helps you accurately measure the specific amount of spirit, liqueur, or juice called for in a cocktail recipe.

One of its cups measures 1oz, the other 2oz. Some types have smaller ¼ and ½oz measurements marked inside the 2oz end.

If you do not own a pony-jigger, however, a standard set of kitchen spoons or a measuring cup are also useful:

3 teaspoons, or 1 tablespoon	= ½oz
4 teaspoons	= ¾oz
2 tablespoons	= 1oz

The recipes in this book are given in ounces for American readers, and in centiliters for readers familiar with metric measurements.

We have worked on the basis that 1oz is equivalent to 3cl, 2oz equals 6cl, and so on.

How many drinks can you get from one bottle? If a bottle contains 70cl, which is approximately 23oz, and a cocktail recipe calls for 5cl, for example, then you can make 14 of that cocktail.

At first, it is a good idea to use the jigger for exact amounts so you gain a good idea of what the cocktails should taste like. As your confidence grows, you might add more of this and a dash of that to change the taste to satisfy your palate. The thing to remember is: Be consistent and retain the proportions.

Unwritten rules among bartenders are that a cocktail should contain no more than 2oz (6cl) of alcohol, and no more than five ingredients. Also, the total volume of a long drink should not be more than 9oz (27cl).

SOME COCKTAIL TERMS

BLEND
To use an electric blender to make a smooth liquid from a fresh, solid ingredient such as fruit, or a heavy juice, coconut cream, or cream.

BUILD
To pour the ingredients directly into the glass.

DASH
A small amount that flows when a bottle is quickly inverted once.

FLOAT
To float one spirit or liqueur over another. Used in Pousse-Café-style drinks (page 90).

MUDDLE
A term meaning to crush with vigor. Muddling is an important part of mixing some classic cocktails that require the use of herbs, such as fresh mint. A muddler lets you grind ingredients in the bottom of the glass without marking the glass (page 62).

NEAT
Serving a drink "straight," without any ice, water, or mixer.

POUSSE-CAFÉ
A drink made of different, usually colorful, layers, built with the heaviest liqueur or spirit poured into the bottom of the glass first, followed by the next lightest, and so on.

SHAKE
Always shake for about 10 seconds. If the recipe calls for cream, shake more sharply. Do not shake a fizzy drink.

STIR
Drinks combined in a mixing glass need just a couple of quick stirs to combine the spirits. A pitcher or jug requires longer—about 15 seconds. When adding lemonade or carbonated water to a cocktail, just stir quickly.

SPIRAL
A thin peel of fruit, such as orange, lemon, or lime, cut in a horizontal direction around the fruit and used either in the drink or as a garnish (page 33).

TWIST
A thin, long strip of peel twisted in the middle and dropped into the drink (see The Martini, page 47).

Glassware

I prefer fine glasses, with thin lips, sparkling and clear. I spend hours looking for the right glass to show off a drink and it is worthwhile for the effect. Glass is certainly preferable to fine china or pewter for cocktails, although if you have just moved, and you can only find the china and the packing box of spirits, don't hesitate to use a cup!

Oh, and here's a tip:

Handle any stemmed glassware by the stem, not the bowl. This helps keep the cocktail chilled.

Clear glasses are best; colored glasses usually only look good if the drink contains clear liquid, although a cocktail with a dominance of cranberry juice poured into a lilac-tinted glass can look OK. But you wouldn't pour a yellow-based cocktail into pale pink-, blue-, or green-tinted glass. It would look muddy.

For a home bar, just a few types are essential.

OLD-FASHIONED

A short glass, ideally with a heavy base so it sits perfectly in the palm of your hand. Used for short cocktails like the classic Negroni (page 58).

HIGHBALL

Used for long drinks and ideally should be wide at the rim. (If it's not, then you can catch your nose when you sip the drink!) Highballs look superb filled with ice, and when you pour in the spirit, it trickles down through the ice, becoming chilled on its way to the bottom of the glass.

a	COCKTAIL	g	SHOT
b	DOUBLE COCKTAIL	h	CHAMPAGNE
c	OLD-FASHIONED	i	RED WINE
d	HIGHBALL	j	MARGARITA
e	LIQUEUR (CORDIAL)	k	CHAMPAGNE FLUTE
f	BEER OR LAGER	l	WHITE WINE

COCKTAIL

These come in a wide range of sizes and prices. Regular-sized cocktail glasses are best for our purposes. Williams–Sonoma, Crate & Barrel, and Jerry's Home Store have good ranges of glassware. However, if you're stuck for a cocktail glass, use a small dessert glass, the type of thing in which you would serve a mousse or zabaglione.

WHITE AND RED WINE

Wine glasses are good for cocktails with a few ingredients, including fruit juices. When buying wine glasses, always look for those with a design on the stem. It adds a visual interest.

GOBLET

Goblets are really the original large wine glass, and are best for exotic cocktails with a lot of color and juice and a big garnish on the side. The drink has power so the glass has to reflect that. Look for goblets with interesting stems, too, and even decorative elements either printed or hand-painted onto the glass.

CHAMPAGNE FLUTE

Champagne flutes look more sophisticated, regardless of whether they are made of crystal, glass, or quality plastic than those shaped like a saucer. (This shape, apparently, was modeled on France's Empress Josephine's breast!) They are reappearing in some stores but true champagne drinkers disdain this shape. They say the champagne goes flat too quickly.

The purpose of a flute is to let you see the bubbles rising up the glass. If you are buying new glasses, look for classic styles with added stem or base interest.

If you don't have champagne glasses, use a tall, thin white wine glass so you don't miss out on the bubble effect.

Getting Organized

On the day that you are going to entertain, it is best to be organized.
The evening will be more relaxing for you as the host (or hostess) if you
do not have to worry about whether you have enough for guests to drink, or have
the right spirits for the cocktails you want to serve. Take a minute to read through this
advice and your party will be more fun!

If an event starts right, it will finish right. If it starts wrong, it will finish wrong. This is a common saying in the catering business! And it is very true.

The organization for a large cocktail party ought to begin at least two to three weeks before the event. The evening will be more entertaining if you can be free to greet and amuse guests and not be concerned about the details.

If you are throwing a party for, say, 20 to 30 people, it is best to decide beforehand which cocktails to offer. Generally, a selection of six is fine. Read through some classic recipes and choose the ones you like most. If you know your guests like vodka, then choose two vodka recipes. If others prefer gin, add a gin-based recipe. White rum is also popular, and there are delicious recipes using white rum, so consider one or two of these, too, for inclusion in your cocktail menu. Tequila, the spirit in such famous classics as Margarita, is also popular. (Avoid Tequila Slammers, as they are potent!)

Consider whether your friends prefer sweet or tart flavors. This will also edit the type of recipes you select. You can choose a selection of both flavors to be safe.

The most important thing is to choose recipes you will feel comfortable making. Recipes that are mixed (built), muddled, and shaken are easiest; the blender is messy and noisy; however, it does result in some delicious cocktails, as you will discover in the blended recipe chapter (page 82).

When you have a definitive cocktail menu, make a list of spirits and mixers you'll need. If you are serving classic Margaritas (page 78), add fine salt for the rim to the list. And a flat saucer. Think about the garnishes you want to add, and make a second list of the types of fruits required for the final touches.

Write a third list of the equipment needed, including a sharp knife and a cutting board. Make sure you have all the right tools for making each drink and its garnish, and a clean kitchen towel to wipe up spills.

The amount of ice you will need differs according to the types of cocktails you are going to make. Buy small bags of ice and place them in your freezer. Six small bags of ice is fine. Fill an ice bucket about five minutes before the guests are expected.

You can prepare cocktails in advance without wasting ingredients. It is important to make sure guests don't have to wait too long for their drinks when they arrive—and that you don't panic or get frustrated. For example, with a Margarita, you can salt the rims of up to 10 glasses beforehand. It will stay on; don't worry. Then pour the recipe's ingredients— tequila, lime juice, and Cointreau—into a pitcher, multiplied by 10. Do not add ice at this stage. Place the pitcher in the refrigerator. As guests arrive, pour the specific amount of mixture for one cocktail into a shaker, add ice cubes, and shake. When you have made a quite few cocktails and are confident, perhaps then you can use your own judgment!

When creating drinks that need muddling, muddle the fruit or mint leaves in advance. Cover the muddled mixture with plastic wrap and place in the refrigerator. This saves time at the mixing stage.

The same applies to garnishes. Prepare each garnish in advance and place in the refrigerator, on a plate, covered with a damp cloth to keep moist. That way you save a lot of fiddling around when guests are lining up for their cocktails.

If the recipe calls for a chilled cocktail glass, make sure you put several in the freezer hours before the event. If you don't have room, put them in the refrigerator, and if there's no room there, don't worry! Fill them with ice a few minutes before adding the drink. The cocktail will be chilled enough when it leaves the shaker. To me, the only time it is imperative to have a chilled glass is if I am serving a Martini (page 44).

The correct glassware does matter at a more formal party. If you do not own a set of Martini cocktail glasses, don't rush out and buy a dozen. It's not expensive to rent glasses, so investigate that option. For an informal party at home, use a variety of shapes—as long as the drink tastes divine, your friends will not notice!

Serving fabulous cocktails with a sense of style also adds an impressive note to an evening. Use a chic tray; one that's not too heavy before the glasses are added, nor too large—and place the glasses upon it without overcrowding them. Serve with care!

For a home bar just a few spirits and mixers are essential.

ESSENTIAL BAR SPIRITS

in order of popularity

vodka

tequila

white rum

gin

bourbon

whiskey

brandy

Campari

Pimm's No. 1 Cup

dry and sweet vermouth

LIQUEURS

Amaretto

Blue Curaçao

Cointreau

Grand Marnier

grenadine

limoncello

crème de menthe
   (white and green)

crème de cacao

WINES

white

red

champagne or sparkling wine

MIXERS

soda water

lemonade

ginger ale

EXTRAS

coconut cream

fine salt

fresh ginger

ground black pepper and salt

light cream

superfine sugar

Tabasco sauce

Worcestershire sauce

JUICES

cranberry

guava

lime

lemon

mango

orange

pineapple

tomato

white and pink grapefruit

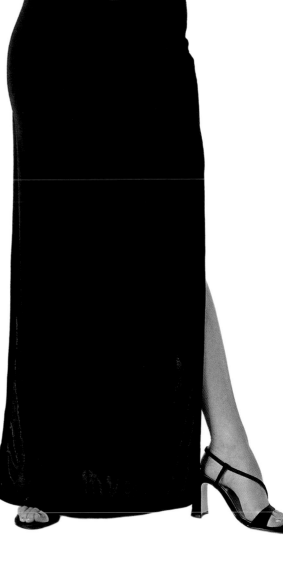

Other Useful Tips

Here are a few general tips that will help you make sense of some ingredients or directions you just might encounter during your journey into the cocktail hour. Master these, and you are well on the way to letting go of some of those wimpish characteristics. . .

HOW TO CHILL A GLASS

Rule number one: Always chill a cocktail glass before you pour any liquid into it. Put the required number of cocktail glasses in the freezer for a few hours before you need to use them. Or, fill them with crushed ice—this will chill them in advance of the final cocktail being poured in. Throw this ice away before adding the drink, though!

HOW TO FROST A RIM

Frosted glasses look fabulous when you present a drink. You'll need a frosted rim for the classic Margarita (page 78). To frost a glass with salt, rub around the rim with a wedge of lemon or lime. Pour a layer of salt onto a flat saucer or small plate. Hold the glass by its stem and dip the rim into the saucer. The salt will stick to the rim. The result will be a superb silvery, crusty rim.

Creating a sugar-frost around the rim is also easy. Take a chilled glass, moisten the rim with a slice of lemon or lime, and dip the rim in a saucer of superfine sugar.

HOW TO USE THE MIXING GLASS

Use a mixing glass to combine spirits and liqueurs (cordials) before pouring them into a cocktail glass.

Always place the ice in the glass first, and stir it around to chill the glass. Strain off any excess water. Add each spirit and stir the mixture vigorously. Strain into the serving glass.

Classic cocktails like the Negroni and the Manhattan are created this way, as you will find in the Easy Mixing chapter (page 48).

HOW TO LAYER

Layered drinks are amazing! Watch anyone's face when you hand them a B-52, a Pousse-Café, or an Irish Coffee (how many times have you had an Irish Coffee which looks like the muddy Mississippi River?) and you will feel pleased that YOU made it (see pages 90 to 97).

Generally, layered drinks are made in shot or liqueur glasses. You need a steady hand and a bar spoon.

Read the label on the spirit or liqueur bottle to find the alcohol volume—the lower it is, the more sugar it contains, and the heavier it will be, like a syrup.

If there are five ingredients in a recipe, such as in a Pousse-Café, begin with the heaviest. To pour the second, less heavy ingredient, pick up the bar spoon and place it in the glass on the edge of the first layer, with the back of the bar spoon facing up.

Pour the next amount carefully onto the highest point of the spoon, and it will gradually flow down to create a second layer. Patience is essential. Repeat the act for each successive lighter layer.

The beauty of a Pousse-Café is that it will hold for about 20 minutes if poured correctly. That's very impressive. Cocktails such as this are a lot of fun—the sad thing is that your guest will gulp it down in one!

Garnishes for Cocktails

These are the finishing touches, the one thing that brings a drink

to your attention. Fashions come and go in garnishes as they do in

other areas. Remember the colorful paper umbrella? I prefer

simple, classic garnishes. This section shows some of my favorite

garnishes, and how to make them. Always use a sharp knife!

Choosing the right garnish requires you to think about the flavor of the drink. For example, you wouldn't add a sweet-tasting fruit garnish to a drink that is distinctly on the tart side. The trick is to match the garnish with the dominating flavor.

The second aspect to consider is the drink's color. Here's a good example: The Mint Julep is clear with a hint of green from the mint. Adding a slice of pineapple ruins the drink. The sweetness seeps into the drink, and you lose the mint flavor. The color also clashes violently, making you wonder about the taste of whoever made the drink!

The appropriate garnish for a Mint Julep is a small sprig of fresh mint.

Pineapple is best used for drinks served in larger glasses, which brings us to the third point to consider. A successful garnish is in proportion to the glass. Three small red currants on a cocktail stick perched on the rim looks silly, whereas a stalk of red currants cascading down from the rim is perfect.

Celery is usually used in a Bloody Mary. Then again, some BM drinkers loathe the stuff. Ask your guest first before adding!

Strawberries are delicious and a favorite of many people, whether dropped in the drink, particularly into a flute of champagne, or perched on the rim. As with all fruit, use only the best-looking ones, smaller rather than larger in size. Take out the green stem, and slice into as many pieces as you want ▶

- Choose a fruit with good skin color. Cut a thin slice through the fruit, no more than a ¼ inch (5mm) thick.
- Pierce it through the middle with a cocktail stick, leaving just enough stick poking through to add a cherry.
- Choose a well-shaped cocktail cherry and slide it onto the cocktail stick until it meets the star fruit.

vertical wedge of pineapple

citrus spiral

red currants

celery stick

star fruit and a maraschino cherry

BLACKBERRY AND MINT GARNISH

without separating them. That way you can fan out the slices (see below) and slip the strawberry over the rim of the glass. Or you can spear the strawberry fan with a cocktail stick and add another fruit, such as a slice of orange.

You can also use a whole hulled strawberry, and make a small slit in the bottom so it can slip over the rim.

Fresh berries such as the blackberry, the blueberry, and the raspberry are good as garnishes. Below, we have added a small sprig of mint to a blackberry and it looks delicious. Try this on one of the nonalcoholic drinks in the last chapter.

Adding more than one fruit to a cocktail stick creates added effect. Adding a spiral of

◀ BERRY GARNISH

- Wash a few blackberries and a sprig of small-leaf mint and pat them dry.
- Make a tiny incision in the top of the berry with the tip of a sharp knife.
- Select a few small mint leaves with a bit of a stem and push the stem into the incision. Spear with a cocktail stick to add to the rim of the glass.

Strawberry Fan

Blackberry Mint

Cherry-Orange Twist

orange or lemon peel around the rim looks even more impressive. All it takes is patience. Here, we have speared three red cherries and entwined them with a thin strip of orange. To make a strip, cut a wide strip of peel around the orange using a zester. Place the peel on a chopping board, holding down each end with your fingers. Using a bar knife, cut a series of thin strips no more than ⅛ inch (3mm) wide. Spear one end onto the cocktail stick and, holding it firmly with one finger, twist the strip around and spear it onto the other end of the stick. Fiddle with it to make sure it twists where you want it to.

Exotic fruits make interesting garnishes. The coolest fancy fruit is the magical Cape Gooseberry—a small orange berry ▶

CAPE GOOSEBERRY

- Hold a washed Cape Gooseberry in your hand.
- Gently unfurl the layers one by one, working the leaf into a shape that reveals the golden orange fruit. Make a small slit in the bottom of the fruit ball to enable it to sit on the rim of the glass.

APPLE SLICE

- Hold a washed apple with a pale skin in one hand and cut a small wedge; put to one side.
- On a red apple, cut a second deeper V-shape. On the pale apple, cut a third deeper V-shape, and put them on top of each other like a puzzle.

Raspberry Trio

Apple Layer

Cape Gooseberry

enveloped in the middle of a series of pale and delicate paper lantern leaves. It has a mild scent and a sharp, tangy flavor. (Eat it dipped in chocolate, too!)

The humble apple looks good as a garnish, too. Using two different colored apples creates a fun decoration. (See steps on previous page.)

Most other fruits can be cut in a simple way. Scoring the peel of lemons, oranges, and limes adds a stylish touch. When cutting wedges or quarters, use the freshest part of the fruit, avoiding any brown marks. When slicing or making wedges, choose fruit that is firm to the touch. And wash the fruit first and dry with a paper towel.

Scored slices of orange, lemon, and lime

Small sprig of baby mint leaves

Slice of star fruit

Slices of kiwifruit

Small wedges of pineapple

Wedges of kiwifruit

KIWIFRUIT SLICES AND WEDGES

- Slice a washed kiwifruit in half. From one half, cut slices no more than ⅛inch (3mm) thick.
- Holding the other half at an angle, cut a series of small wedges.
- Leave the skin on for a more sturdy slice.

MAKING A CITRUS SPIRAL

- Wash and pat dry one small citrus fruit, for example, a lime.
- Using a zester, starting from the top, slowly cut around the lime, making a long spiral.
- Hold the lime firmly in your hand and press the zester firmly into the peel. This requires a strong hand and a bit of practice to make the perfect spiral.

Shaking It Up

Shaking. . . for me, it's like playing music. The shaker is my musical instrument. The action is like a hand-samba, raising the level of energy all around. In this section you will find a guide on how to hold the shaker to get the best out of it.

There are two styles of shaker: The Boston shaker, which is popular among professional bartenders, and the three-piece metal shaker, available from most housewares stores.

THE THREE-PIECE SHAKER

This consists of a base, a section with a strainer, and a small lid. It's compact and easy to handle. If the top becomes stuck to the bottom section, ease it up with your thumbs. Sometimes a quick, hard twist will do the trick. You can also try wiping the sides down with a warm, wet cloth. This warms the sides slightly and loosens the vacuum created by the cold and the ice friction.

THE TWO-PIECE BOSTON SHAKER

This shaker is made of two pieces—one is metal, the other is clear glass. It dates from the early days of cocktails, and was seen around in the drinking bars during the '20s and '30s. Now, it is considered part of the true professional bartender's tool kit.

Put the ingredients in the glass section so you can see how much you are using. Add ice. Then pick up the metal part and cover the glass, gently sealing the two with a slap of the palm of your hand. You will notice that it nearly always sits at a sideways angle,

although when we photographed this, it fitted perfectly straight! Now, turn the shaker upside down. This is so when the drink is shaken, the liquid ends up in the metal part. Let the drink settle for a few seconds before opening the shaker.

TO LOOSEN THE SHAKER
Place the shaker on the bar top with the metal section as the base. When you look at the shaker, you'll see the glass is at a slight angle. To break the seal, avoid slapping it at the most angled section. Slap it gently on the side where the line is more vertical. This will release the air vacuum inside.

ESSENTIAL NOTE

Always refill the shaker with fresh ice after making individual drinks. Otherwise you might taint the flavor of the next drink.

The strainer (below) is a separate item. This is an important tool because it holds back any ice and fruit when you pour a cocktail into a glass.

Shaking Sense

I don't shake the shaker as if I am hitting someone with a hammer, almost battering the drink into submission. I like to think you can shake a drink with a certain style.

Hands together, clutch the shaker at around head height, holding the top firmly.

Hold your hand firmly over the cap and the main section, with the top facing up and away from guests. You do not want to spray them!

Now to the exciting part—preparing to shake. The objective is not to separate the two sections when shaking. Always make sure you hold the lid down firmly. You can get carried away and forget this important detail! And a leaking shaker makes a mess everywhere.

Always move the shaker in an up-and-down direction, not sideways. Imagine you have a pair of maracas in your hands and get a rhythm going. Listen to the music of the ice.

As you shake, count to 10. Don't rock the drink to death—on the other hand, don't rock the drink to sleep. You've got to wake it up, energizing the ingredients to combine well.

Obviously, you have to feel comfortable when you hold the shaker in your hands, so practice the position shown here until you feel it is second nature.

Flick the shaker with
your wrists, not your
elbows, away from
the body; listening to
the movement of the
ice and liquids as they
work their magic.

Finally, flick the
shaker with the
wrists back into the
shoulder area,
keeping it upright to
keep both sections
firmly joined to
prevent leakage.

Blending Cocktails

Blended drinks are delicious for all seasons—it doesn't have to be summer! Many of today's exotic cocktails owe their existence to the development of the humble kitchen blender, and mixologists continue to experiment with fruit, cream, and spirits to discover how many more delicious combinations they can create.

FRUITS THAT BLEND WELL

Banana

Blackberry

Blueberry

Kiwifruit

Mango

Raspberry

Strawberry

Hey, you did see the classic movie, *Cocktail*? The beach, Tom Cruise, Bryan Brown, the girls, the ocean, the blender behind the bar...remember? Without the blender there would be no Frozen Daiquiri, no Frozen Margarita, and no Piña Colada (page 86).

Blended cocktails are delicious, combining the texture of fruit with the essence of the spirit. They are colorful, imbued with a sense of fun, giving the imbiber a taste sensation. It is wise not to drink too many because the alcohol is disguised in the other ingredients.

They're also the type of cocktail you can be exuberant with when creating a garnish.

Read the recipe to determine the order in which the ingredients should be put into the blender. Usually, liquid ingredients are added first, and these can be measured either by the jigger or, in the case of larger amounts of fruit juice, by the markings on the side of a liquid measuring cup.

FAVORITE BLENDS

Blue Hawaiian

Cococabana

Frozen Daiquiri

Frozen Margarita

Love in the Afternoon

Piña Colada

True Love

Fruit can be bought in fresh, fresh frozen, and canned forms. The amount of frozen fruit used will cut down the amount of ice needed. And frozen fruit can be much harder to blend, so it is preferable not to resort to the freezer unless you have to! When choosing fruit for the blender, look for softer pieces and beware of fruit that might be soft, but is bruised and does not look fresh. This type of fruit leaves a peculiar taste in a drink.

Canned fruit is also more liquid than fresh fruit, so take this into consideration. Drain for an hour or so before adding it to the blender.

When adding ice to the blender, remember that not all ice is the same. Each type contains a varying amount of air and will react differently in a blender. Measure the amount of ice for the blender by the size of the glass in which the drink is to be served. That way, there will not be too much ice in the drink to water it down!

Timing is also important. No more than a few seconds—10 at the most is fine. Fruit needs to be thoroughly mashed and to have enough time to absorb the spirits. And vice versa.

If you are having a cocktail party for more than 10 to 12 people, the question is how much to make for how many? Not everybody will want to drink the same cocktail, but then again, they might! Usually a recipe is for one drink, but it is sometimes best to make two or more drinks at one time in the blender.

Blended cocktails are best made and served immediately. You can blend the fruits and spirit before an event, and place in a bowl in the refrigerator, but it is best not to add creamy ingredients until the last minute. And, of course, always add the ice last.

Some blended recipes also require the mixture to be strained, making a liquid with a finer texture. This is easy to do. Place a strainer over the glass and pour small amounts of the mixture into the strainer. With a teaspoon or bar spoon, mash the mixture until you can see most of the liquid has passed through the holes in the wire mesh. Then discard the remaining pits or flesh and pour in an additional amount, repeating the process until the glass is filled.

And, remember always to wash the blender thoroughly after making each recipe. It's very important not to taint a new flavor with the leftover taste from the cocktail before.

However, the most important rule of blended cocktails is—enjoy drinking them!

POURING BLENDED COCKTAILS

Since you usually make blended cocktails for more than one person, it is important to share the mixture equally! The trick is to pour a little of the mixture into each glass, then begin pouring again until each glass contains the same amount of liquid.

Above, champagne is being poured into glasses containing mixture from a blender to create the new cocktail, True Love. The art of pouring is in retaining the correct ratio of mixture to champagne in both champagne flutes.

Savoring the Flavor

When making any cocktail, it is important to balance the flavors

in the recipe. To help you understand the importance of flavor

and to guide you through the tasting maze, here are a few points

that are worth your consideration before you select a cocktail.

There are four categories of flavor in a cocktail—sweet, sharp, spicy, and bitter.

The perfect cocktail is the result of a harmony of all four previously mentioned flavors. Before examining them individually, let's look at the most important aspect in the creation of a cocktail—the use of ingredients that do not fight each other, or cancel each other out.

Before you choose which cocktail to make, think about what you want from the drink. Each of us has taste buds that are satisfied by entirely different flavors. Think carefully about what presses your taste buttons, then examine the separate ingredients. For example, if you drink a vodka sour you might think it contains nothing but tartness. Yet, there is a sweetness underlying the flavor. This sweetness balances the sharpness—

without sweetness, the cocktail would be acid and most unpleasant to drink.

Read through a selection of recipes and note their ingredients. Analyze which is sweet and which is sour, and then look at the amount of each required in the recipe. After a while, you will begin to understand the way in which the flavors of each cocktail are balanced.

So, once you have learned the art of balancing flavors, experiment and create the same drink customized to suit individual palates. By that I mean if you prefer a slightly sweeter taste, then add a little extra dash of the sweet ingredient. The same principle applies if you prefer a slightly tart taste: Add a little more lemon or lime juice. Experiment until the cocktail is perfect for you. If you are making the cocktail for others, however, ask how they prefer it and tailor it to their palate.

But remember, until you have mixed a cocktail recipe as given in this book, you will not know exactly how the drink should taste, so do it correctly the first few times, and then experiment.

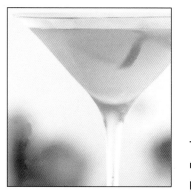

The Cosmopolitan (page 74) is now considered the most popular flavor in the world.

THE FOUR FLAVORS

SWEET

Sweetness in cocktails usually comes from ingredients such as liqueurs—Kahlúa, Cointreau, Bailey's, Grand Marnier, Galliano, and limoncello—which contain an intensity of sugar. These are low in alcohol volume, but high in sugar content.

A Piña Colada, although it doesn't contain a liqueur, tastes sweet because of its pineapple juice and coconut cream. Some after-dinner drinks are recognizably sweet: Sweet Sue (above, and page 104), and any of the layered drinks, such as B-52 (93), and Pousse-Café (96).

SHARP

Sharpness is a flavor that sends shivers down your spine. "Lip-smacking" is also an accurate description. Sharpness refreshes your taste buds more than some other flavors. Any recipe made with fresh lime or lemon juice will taste sharp, as will a drink containing raspberries, which have a distinctly sharp taste. Cocktails with a sharp flavor include Margarita (above, and page 78), Bourbon Smash (page 65), and Raspberry Mint Daiquiri (page 80).

SPICY

Spicy cocktails are those with just a hint of cinnamon or nutmeg, which is either added to the drink or on top of a layer of cream, such as in a Brandy Alexander. Cloves in a perfect cold-winter's-day mulled wine provide a warming, spicy flavor. The classic Bloody Mary (above, and page 52) is spicy because it contains tomato juice, Tabasco sauce, Worcestershire sauce, and ground black pepper.

BITTER

Bitterness is found in cocktails containing Campari and Angostura bitters. Generally, bitterness comes with an ingredient made of herbal extracts, such as Fernet Branca (an excellent digestif). It's been described as an elegant flavor; one that lingers as you sip a cocktail, quenching your thirst. Bitter drinks include Negroni (page 58), and Sea Breeze (page 59).

The

Recipes

the

I've chosen the Martini as a classic feature because it is simple to make, believe it or not. There are two ingredients: vodka (or gin, if you prefer), and dry vermouth. The garnish is an olive or a twist of lemon.

The modern Martini has changed from dry to fruity in style, and there are many different recipes, ranging from the Breakfast Martini made with marmalade to the Blueberry Martini made with the juice of fresh blueberries. On the following pages, however, I reveal how to make the perfect classic Martini.

martini

Martini

INGREDIENTS

2¾oz / 8cl   frozen vodka

1 to 2 drops   extra-dry vermouth

AND . . .

chilled cocktail glass

lemon for garnish

chopping board and bar knife

This is my vodka Martini, yet there are those who prefer a gin Martini. If you know these people, substitute gin for vodka. Here's a tip: I keep the vodka in the freezer, and an hour before guests are expected, I add the glasses to chill. A great Martini is one that stays very cold while you drink it.

1 Take the chilled martini glass from the freezer, handling it by the stem only. Pour the frozen vodka directly into the glass. Fill a glass pourer with extra-dry vermouth and shake a few drops of vermouth into the glass. This way it lays on top of the spirit.

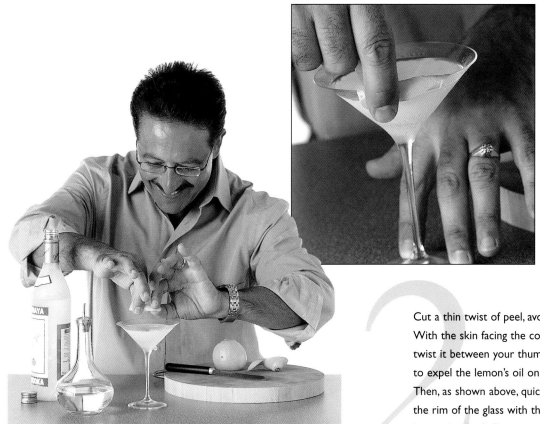

Cut a thin twist of peel, avoiding any pith. With the skin facing the cocktail, squeeze and twist it between your thumb and forefinger to expel the lemon's oil on top of the drink. Then, as shown above, quickly wipe around the rim of the glass with the twist and drop it into the drink. Serve immediately.

easy

mixing

The basic tools for recipes in this section are solid ice cubes, a mixing glass, a strainer, a spirit measure, and a bar spoon. Individual recipes indicate the type of glass, any extra equipment you need, and a simple, stylish garnish that sets off each cocktail.

Blue Monday

INGREDIENTS

⅔oz / 2cl	gin
1⅓oz / 4cl	Cointreau
	soda water
dash	Blue Curaçao

AND . . .

highball glass and stirrer

chopping board and sharp knife

star fruit for garnish

1

Pour the gin, Cointreau, and soda water into the glass filled with ice. Pour a few drops of Blue Curaçao over a bar spoon into the glass. Stir.

2

Cut a small slit in a slice of star fruit and sit the slice on the rim. Serve with the stirrer.

Caruso

INGREDIENTS

1⅔oz / 5cl	gin
1oz / 3cl	dry vermouth
½oz / 1.5cl	green crème de menthe

AND . . .

chilled cocktail glass

strainer

1

Pour ingredients into a
mixing glass filled with ice.
Stir with a bar spoon.

2

Holding the strainer
firmly, strain into the
chilled cocktail glass.

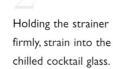

Bloody Mary

Making a Bloody Mary is like cooking a very fine steak. Always ask your guests how they like theirs. At its best, it is a long, cool, and refreshing drink. Adding Tabasco sauce is optional—some people do not like the spicy flavor it brings to the cocktail, so use it upon request.

INGREDIENTS

1¾oz / 5cl	vodka
⅔oz / 2cl	fresh lemon juice
5½oz / 15cl	tomato juice
pinch	celery salt
2 dashes	Worcestershire sauce
1 to 2 dashes	Tabasco sauce
	ground black pepper

AND . . .

highball glass and stirrer

juicer

chopping board and sharp knife

lime for garnish

Celery is the traditional garnish. Here, a wedge of lime was used—a more modern addition.

1 This drink is built directly into the highball. Fill the glass with ice cubes, then pour in the lemon juice.

2 Pour in the tomato juice. Add the vodka. Finally, add the salt and two sauces.

3 Add a twist of black pepper. Garnish with a wedge of lime, adding a celery stalk if you prefer. Or, just add a stirrer.

Kiss on the Lips

INGREDIENTS

2oz / 6cl   bourbon

5oz / 15cl   apricot juice

AND . . .

highball glass and stirrer

1

Pour the bourbon and apricot juice directly into the highball filled with ice, using a bar spoon to stir.

2

Stir until the two liquids are combined well. Serve with a stirrer. A straw is optional.

Knickerbocker

INGREDIENTS

1½oz /5cl	gin
½oz /1.5cl	sweet vermouth
¾oz /2cl	dry vermouth

AND . . .

chilled cocktail glass

chopping board and sharp knife

lemon for twist

1

Pour the gin and both vermouths directly into a mixing glass filled with ice. Stir with a bar spoon. Strain into the chilled cocktail glass.

2

Cut a strip of lemon peel and twist over the drink, then drop it in.

Manhattan

INGREDIENTS

1¾oz / 5cl   Canadian Club whisky

⅔oz / 2cl   sweet vermouth

dash   Angostura bitters

AND . . .

chilled cocktail glass

maraschino cherry for garnish

The Manhattan is a classic cocktail synonymous with the island of

Manhattan. I dedicate this cocktail to the spirit of New Yorkers.

1

Pour the ingredients into
a mixing glass filled with
ice and stir quickly. Strain
into the chilled glass.

2

Drop a maraschino cherry
into the drink!

Negroni

INGREDIENTS

1oz / 3cl	Campari
1oz / 3cl	gin
1oz / 3cl	sweet vermouth
	soda water (optional)

AND . . .

old-fashioned glass and stirrer

chopping board and sharp knife

orange for garnish

1

Pour the ingredients directly into the old-fashioned glass filled with ice. Stir, add soda water if preferred.

The important trick to this cocktail is to make sure you measure the ingredients exactly. That way, you guarantee the balanced flavor.

2

Garnish with a slice of orange dropped into the drink. Add a stirrer.

Sea Breeze

1

Pour the cranberry juice and then the vodka into a highball filled with ice. Stir. Add the grapefruit juice.

INGREDIENTS

1¾oz / 5cl   vodka
13½oz / 10cl   cranberry juice
1¾oz / 5cl   fresh grapefruit juice

AND . . .

highball glass and stirrer
chopping board and sharp knife
lime for garnish

2

Garnish with a wedge of lime. Serve with a stirrer.

Tequila Sunrise

Aaah, remember when the sun came up on the beach during your vacation? Well, now you can mix this refreshing drink and recall that very moment. Remember a dash is a quick pour!

1

Pour the tequila and orange juice into the highball filled with ice and stir. Add a dash of grenadine so it sinks slowly down through the ice and liquids.

INGREDIENTS

1¾oz / 5cl   tequila
5½oz / 15cl   fresh orange juice
1 to 2 dashes   grenadine

AND . . .

highball glass and stirrer

juicer

orange

chopping board and sharp knife

zester

orange for garnish

MAKING THE SLICE AND SPIRAL

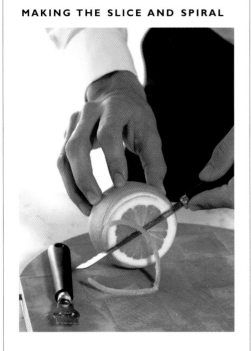

• Cut an orange in half. Using a zester, cut a thin spiral of peel to almost full circle.

• Place the knife in the middle of the orange and cut crosswise, making half a slice with the spiral attached.

2 Lay the slice of orange on top of the drink, with the spiral hanging over the rim. Serve with a stirrer. A straw is optional.

For each of these recipes you need a muddler, a spirit measure, and a bar spoon. Every recipe, except the Caipirinha, uses crushed ice. Mostly, things like berry fruits or mint leaves are muddled directly in an old-fashioned or a highball glass with a heavy base. Ingredients are sometimes muddled in a shaker (without ice).

Muddling is a simple action requiring strength in the wrist. More bartenders are using this technique—it brings out the essence while the freshness of the fruit remains intact. Some bar spoons have a muddler attached, but the best results come from using a wooden muddler!

muddle

it . . . .

Berry Nice

INGREDIENTS

2oz / 6cl	cachaça
2	small limes
1 tablespoon	brown sugar
6	strawberries, stems removed, and diced
5 or 6	blueberries
5 or 6	raspberries

AND . . .

old-fashioned glasses

small glass mixing bowl and tablespoon

short straws

This recipe, an updated version of the

Caipirinha (page 67), makes two cocktails.

1

Wash the limes and cut them into small segments. Add the sugar and limes to the mixing bowl. Muddle the limes, releasing the juices, then add the berries. Continue to muddle until the juices run freely.

2

Place one spoonful into each glass. Add the cachaça and crushed ice to each. Stir. Serve this cocktail with a short straw to stir the drink.

Bourbon Smash

INGREDIENTS

1¾oz / 5cl	bourbon
1	small lime, diced
handful	fresh raspberries
½ teaspoon	superfine sugar
dash	Angostura bitters
2⅓oz / 7cl	cranberry juice

AND . . .

large old-fashioned glass
red currants for garnish

This cocktail has sharpness, an aromatic flavor provided by the strength of the bourbon, the freshness of raspberry, and the tart taste of cranberry.

1

Place the diced lime and raspberries in the bottom of the glass, then add the sugar and bitters. Muddle well to dissolve the sugar and bitters.

2

Add the measure of bourbon, then the crushed ice, and top up with cranberry juice. Garnish with a sprig of red currants balanced on the rim.

Bramble

Also known as Gin Bramble, one stir and the soda disappears into this deep-red cocktail with a delicious flavor of fresh blackberries.

INGREDIENTS

1⅔oz /5cl	gin
4	blackberries
juice of	1 lime
1 teaspoon	superfine sugar
	soda water
dash	crème de mur (blackberry liqueur)

AND . . .

highball glass and stirrer

small mixing bowl

juicer for lime juice

small strainer

berry and sprig of mint for garnish

1

Place the blackberries in a bowl. Add the lime juice and superfine sugar. Muddle. Strain into the glass to extract all the juices.

2

Add the gin and crushed ice. Top up with soda water. Add the crème de mur. Stir. Garnish with a blackberry with a small sprig of mint placed on the rim.

Caipirinha

1

Wash the lime, remove the top and the bottom, and cut into small pieces. Add both the sugar and pieces of lime to a bowl.

INGREDIENTS

1⅔oz /5cl   cachaça

1   small lime, diced

1½ teaspoons   brown sugar

AND . . .

old-fashioned glass and stirrer

small bowl

chopping board and sharp knife

ice cubes and scoop

2

Crush the lime with the muddler to make as much juice as possible and to make sure the sugar dissolves.

3

Transfer the mixture to the old-fashioned glass, add dry ice cubes and pour in the cachaça. Stir. Serve with a stirrer.

Mint Julep

INGREDIENTS

1¾oz / 5cl	bourbon
bunch	fresh mint leaves
1 teaspoon	superfine sugar
1 tablespoon	cold water

AND . . .

old-fashioned glass

This recipe makes one drink. To make a pitcher of julep, multiply the ingredients by the number of people drinking.

1

Place the mint in the glass. Add the sugar and water. Crush with the back of a bar spoon until the sugar dissolves and the fragrance of the mint is released.

2

Add the bourbon. Fill the glass with crushed ice. Stir. Garnish with a sprig of mint.

Pink Mojito

INGREDIENTS

1¾oz /5cl	white rum
1 teaspoon	superfine sugar
juice of	1 lime
3 sprigs	fresh mint leaves on stems
dash	cranberry juice
	soda water

AND . . .

highball glass and stirrer

small pitcher for pouring cranberry juice

juicer for lime juice

stirrer

This is a modern version of a classic cocktail, the Mojito, created by adding cranberry juice. A real thirst-quencher for summer days.

1

Put the sugar and lime juice in the bottom of the glass. Add the mint leaves and muddle.

2

Add the rum, then fill the glass with crushed ice. Add a few fresh mint leaves. Top up with soda water. Add a dash of cranberry juice. Stir. Serve with a stirrer.

shake

it...

Shaking a drink combines the spirit thoroughly with the juice or other ingredients, such as cream, and also chills the drink. Add solid ice cubes to a shaker to about three-quarters full. Make the cocktail, discard the ice cubes, and rinse before making another drink using fresh ice cubes. Don't forget to use the spirit measure!

Amalfi Dream

INGREDIENTS

1¾oz /5cl	vodka
⅔oz /2cl	limoncello
juice of	half a lemon
4 to 5 leaves	fresh mint

AND . . .

chilled cocktail glass

juicer

strainer

chopping board and sharp knife for lemon peel garnish

1 Pour the vodka and limoncello into a shaker filled with dry ice cubes. Add several mint leaves. Shake vigorously for at least 10 seconds to let the flavor of the mint infuse with the limoncello and lemon. The mint leaves will be broken into fragments by the ice.

This cocktail was mixed with a creamy limoncello, but you can make it with regular limoncello, too. I wanted to create a flavor contrast between the sharpness of lemon juice and the sweetness of limoncello.

2 Strain into a chilled cocktail glass, allowing some of the mint fragments to slip through with the drink for a speckled effect. Make a strip of lemon peel for the garnish and let it hang over the rim.

Cosmopolitan

INGREDIENTS

1¾oz / 5cl	vodka
⅓oz / 1cl	Cointreau
⅓oz / 1cl	cranberry juice
⅓oz / 1cl	fresh lime juice

AND . . .

chilled cocktail glass

juicer

zester for orange garnish

1 Pour all the ingredients into a shaker filled with ice cubes. Shake sharply. Strain into a chilled cocktail glass.

2 Take the orange in one hand and, using a zester, cut a thin spiral to make into a twist.

The Cosmopolitan is the most delectable modern cocktail to hit the taste buds in recent years. A delicious contrast in flavors is provided by tart fresh lime juice and sweet Cointreau. It is securely in first place in the history of modern classic cocktails.

3 Squeeze the twist over the drink to release the essences and then drop it into the drink. Serve.

Dolce Havana

INGREDIENTS

1⅓oz / 4cl	white rum
⅔oz / 2cl	Aperol
½oz / 1.5cl	Cointreau
1oz / 3cl	fresh orange juice
⅔oz / 2cl	fresh lime juice

AND . . .

chilled cocktail glass

juicer

sharp knife to make a slit in the Cape
Gooseberry garnish

1

Make the orange and
lime juices. Pour all ingredients
into a shaker filled with ice.
Shake and salsa simultaneously.

2

Strain into a chilled
cocktail glass.
Cut a slit into a
Cape Gooseberry
and place it on
the rim.

La Bomba

INGREDIENTS

1⅓oz /4cl	gold tequila
⅔oz /2cl	Cointreau
1⅓oz /4cl	pineapple juice
1⅓oz /4cl	orange juice
2 dashes	grenadine

AND . . .

wine goblet or cocktail glass

spirit pourer

saucer and superfine sugar for coating the rim

chopping board and sharp knife for orange garnish

1

Pour all ingredients into a shaker with ice cubes. Shake quickly. Coat the rim of a chilled glass with a slice of orange and dip in a saucer of superfine sugar.

2

Strain into a glass and add two dashes of grenadine. Cut a slice of orange as a garnish and place on the rim.

Margarita

INGREDIENTS

1oz / 3cl	silver tequila
⅔oz / 2cl	Cointreau
1oz / 3cl	fresh lime juice

AND . . .

margarita or large wine glass

saucer and salt for coating the rim

chopping board and sharp knife for
lime garnish

1

Rub the rim of the
glass with a slice of
lime to prepare it for
the salt.

2

Dip the glass in a saucer with
a layer of fine salt. The salt
will adhere to the sticky rim,
forming a crust.

The Margarita has been with us for many decades and is still very popular. If you don't have a Margarita glass, pick one with an interesting shape from your own collection, like the wine glass shown here.

3 Pour all ingredients into a shaker with ice cubes. Shake sharply. Strain into a glass. Cut a slice of lime for the garnish and add to the rim.

Raspberry Mint Daiquiri

INGREDIENTS

1¾oz / 5cl	white rum
handful	fresh raspberries
6 leaves	fresh mint

AND . . .

chilled cocktail glass

extra strainer to catch mint pieces

cocktail stick, 2 raspberries, and a tiny sprig of mint for garnish

1

Place all the ingredients into a shaker with ice cubes. Shake vigorously to let the flavor of the mint infuse, and the raspberries to be pulverized. Strain into a chilled cocktail glass.

2

Garnish with two raspberries and a sprig of mint on a cocktail stick placed across the glass.

Stiletto

INGREDIENTS

1½oz /4.5cl   bourbon

1½oz /4.5cl   Amaretto

juice of   1 lime

AND . . .

chilled cocktail glass

juicer

chopping board and sharp knife for lime garnish

1

Cut lime in half and squeeze over a juicer. Pour all the ingredients into a shaker filled with ice cubes. Shake. Strain into the chilled cocktail glass.

2

Cut a thin wedge of lime and make a slit in the flesh so it sits on the rim.

SHAKE IT

For these recipes, you need a blender, ice bucket and scoop, crushed ice, and a spirit measure. Be careful when you add the crushed ice—follow the instructions for when to add it! Serve a blended cocktail quickly because it can "separate" and lose its initial visual effect!

Blend

it . . . .

Maria

INGREDIENTS

1oz / 3cl	tequila
½oz / 1.5cl	Tia Maria
½oz / 1.5cl	crème de banane
half	fresh banana
1oz / 3cl	heavy (double) cream

AND . . .

pilsner or colada glass

ice bucket and scoop

3 coffee beans for garnish

1

Place all of the ingredients into a blender. Blend until smooth. Add two scoops of crushed ice. Blend for five seconds more.

2

Pour into the glass. Place two or three coffee beans on top. Serve with a clear straw if you prefer.

Maui Breeze

INGREDIENTS

½oz / 1.5cl	Amaretto
½oz / 1.5cl	Cointreau
½oz / 1.5cl	brandy
2oz / 6cl	orange juice
2oz / 6cl	guava juice
juice of	half a lemon
1 teaspoon	superfine sugar

AND . . .

highball or colada glass

ice bucket and scoop

cocktail stick, slice of lime, and maraschino cherry for garnish

With this recipe, the ice is put in the blender at the same time as the other ingredients. This is because no solid ingredient needs to be mashed first.

1

Put two or three scoops of crushed ice into a blender. Add all the other ingredients and blend until smooth.

2

Pour into the highball. Garnish with a slice of lime and a maraschino cherry speared by a cocktail stick. Or, add a small slipper orchid flower to make the drink look more Hawaiian....

Piña Colada

The most famous of the coladas is the Piña Colada—its name means "strained pineapple." This exotic number originated in Puerto Rico, and there are fans who will drink no other summer cocktail. Use the freshest top-quality fruit you can buy. When blended, all of the drink should be milky white, not separated into clear liquid and opaque froth.

1

Pour the pineapple juice (or the three slices of pineapple) into the blender. Add the coconut cream and the white rum. Blend for a few seconds. Add the crushed ice and blend for 5 seconds. Pour into the glass.

Blue Hawaiian

2

Garnish with a wedge of fresh pineapple, two short pineapple leaves, and a maraschino cherry speared by a cocktail stick placed across the glass.

This cocktail is a Piña Colada with a blue spark. Just add a dash or two—no more than ⅔oz/2cl—of Blue Curaçao to the blender. Serve a cream and a blue cocktail together!

Sydney Sling

INGREDIENTS

1¾oz / 5cl	white rum
⅔oz / 2cl	cherry brandy
few dashes	peach schnapps
2⅓oz / 7cl	guava juice
2⅓oz / 7cl	pineapple juice
juice of	half a lemon
	half a banana

AND . . .

large wine glass or goblet

ice bucket and scoop

sharp knife to cut a slit in a Cape
Gooseberry for garnish

1

Place all the ingredients into the
blender and blend for a few
seconds to let the banana
mash. Add two
scoops of crushed
ice and blend. Pour
into the glass.

2

Hold a Cape Gooseberry in one hand and
gently tear down along the fragile veins to
make a series of small leaves. Pull all of the
leaves away from the fruit as above. Cut a
slit in the bottom of the fruit and place on
the rim. Shape the leaves into place.

True Love

INGREDIENTS

⅔oz / 2cl   Grand Marnier

dash   brandy

       champagne

5 to 6   strawberries, minus stems
       and cut in half

AND . . .

chilled champagne flutes

sharp knife to cut slit in strawberries

extra strawberries and small sprig of fresh
mint for garnish

Advance preparation: Blend the strawberries, Grand Marnier, and brandy for a few moments until smooth. Place in a covered container in the refrigerator for a few hours to chill.

1

Pour the chilled fruit mixture into each chilled champagne flute until about a quarter full, then add the champagne in a measured way so that each drink is level.

2

Stir gently, almost lifting the liquid: You don't want to create a froth. Garnish with a strawberry and a small sprig of mint set on the rim.

Although these cocktails look a little difficult, they are not. You need a steady hand, a good eye—and concentration as you pour each layer. Essential tools are a bar spoon and a spirit pourer for the bottle. The trick is to remember that spirits and cordials have different alcohol volumes. The lower the alcohol volume, the more sugar there is and the heavier the spirit. Pour the heaviest followed by lighter spirits and create brilliant layers!

layer

it . . . .

American Flag

INGREDIENTS

¾oz /2.5cl   crème de fraise

¾oz /2.5cl   Cointreau

¾oz /2.5cl   frozen vodka

2 to 3 dashes   Blue Curaçao

AND . . .

port or liqueur glass

mixing glass

This is the perfect cocktail at the end of a Fourth of July party!

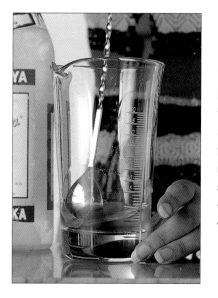

1

Place the glass on a clean and level counter top. Add the crème de fraise. Using the back of a bar spoon, carefully add the Cointreau to make a second clear layer. In a mixing glass, mix the frozen vodka and two to three dashes of Blue Curaçao. Stir quickly to turn the vodka blue.

2

Gently layer this on top of the Cointreau. That's it!

B–52

INGREDIENTS

⅔oz /2cl   Kahlúa

⅔oz /2cl   Bailey's Irish Cream

⅔oz /2cl   Grand Marnier

AND . . .

liqueur glass

1

Pour the Kahlúa into the glass first. Over the back of a bar spoon, slowly pour the Bailey's to create a second creamy layer.

2

After a small pause, pour the Grand Marnier over the back of the bar spoon to create the final layer. Sip slowly to enjoy all of the flavors. Or, gulp it down to experience the intense mix of flavors in the mouth! Wow!

Irish Coffee

INGREDIENTS

1oz / 3cl	Irish whiskey
1 teaspoon	raw sugar
	hot, strong coffee
	heavy (double) cream

AND . . .

warm wine glass or small glass mug

small pitcher for pouring cream

1

Warm a wine glass with hot water. Dry. Put the sugar and whiskey into the glass and stir to dissolve the sugar. Stir in the coffee.

2

Float the cream over the back of a bar spoon to layer it over the coffee. Serve. Drink the coffee through the cream.

Peach Haze

INGREDIENTS

¾oz / 2.5cl	frozen peach schnapps
¾oz / 2.5cl	cranberry juice
¾oz / 2.5cl	frozen vodka

AND . . .

frozen shot glass

Freezing the vodka and peach schnapps adds an extra touch to the presentation of this lightly colored cocktail—a great mix of sweet and tart flavors in one short hit!

1

Freeze a bottle of peach schnapps and a shot glass in the freezer before you make the drink to create a frosted effect.

2

Pour the peach schnapps into the frozen shot glass. Using the back of a bar spoon, carefully pour the cranberry juice over the schnapps. When that has settled, add the vodka.

Pousse-Café

INGREDIENTS

⅓oz / 1cl	grenadine
⅓oz / 1cl	green crème de menthe
⅓oz / 1cl	Galliano
⅓oz / 1cl	Kümmel
⅓oz / 1cl	brandy

AND . . .

shot glass

Amanda found it was easier when she concentrated on pouring each layer, making sure the liquid hit the top of the back of the bar spoon. Using a spirit pourer in the top of the bottle is essential. You, too, can do it!

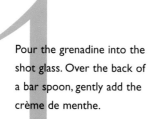

Pour the grenadine into the shot glass. Over the back of a bar spoon, gently add the crème de menthe.

2 Pause, add the Galliano the same way. Pause, add the Kümmel.

3 Finally add the brandy. Serve carefully. If you move the glass quickly, you will upset the perfect dividing lines!

In this chapter I am going to help you make unique cocktails for the important people in your life.

First, ask which spirits they prefer. Then, what's their favorite color? You've got quite a color range to choose from, when you survey the colors of liqueurs and fruit juices available. Now, flavor. Do they prefer dry or semidry, sweet, or sour tastes? Do they like a long and refreshing drink, or short and sweet with a kick? Personality is another element: Are they effervescent, with a great smile? If so, champagne is a must. Exotic? Then use ingredients such as guava, passionfruit, and mango juices. Or Blue Curaçao to remind them of a turquoise ocean.

And, the cocktail's name. It should reflect the person. If they have a sense of humor, it can be witty!

Some of these cocktails are shaken, others mixed. The tools needed are listed under each recipe, as is the type of ice required. A spirit measure is essential.

personality

cocktails

Mac Martini

1¾oz / 5cl	gin
⅓oz / 1cl	Blue Curaçao
⅓oz / 1cl	Midori melon liqueur
1 teaspoon	champagne

AND . . .

chilled cocktail glass

shaker filled with ice cubes

bar spoon

cocktails for wimps

1

Pour all the ingredients, except the champagne, into a cocktail shaker. Shake. Strain into the chilled cocktail glass. Gently float the champagne on top for a sparkling, dry finish. Note Stevan is using the spoon with the bowl facing up—he finds it easier to float bubbling liquids this way.

Meg's Mania

INGREDIENTS

1⅔oz / 5cl	vodka
⅓oz / 1cl	rice wine (sake)
⅓oz / 1cl	cranberry juice
juice of	one lime
	champagne

AND . . .

shaker filled with ice cubes

chilled champagne flute

chopping board and zester for making lime garnish

1

Pour the ingredients, except the champagne, into a shaker. Shake. Strain into the chilled flute. Top up with champagne. Make the lime spiral garnish with a zester. Set this on the rim of the glass.

Peta's Passion

INGREDIENTS

1⅔oz / 5cl	tequila
2⅓oz / 7cl	apple juice
juice of	1 small lime
1 teaspoon	superfine sugar
1⅔oz / 5cl	passionfruit juice

AND . . .

highball glass filled with crushed ice; stirrer

shaker filled with ice cubes

bar spoon

chopping board and sharp knife for passionfruit garnish

1

Pour all the ingredients into a shaker. Shake. Strain into the highball filled with crushed ice.

2

Scoop out the pulp of the passionfruit and lay it on top of the drink: It gives it a piquant aroma. Serve with a stirrer.

Red Earl

INGREDIENTS

1¾oz /5cl	vodka
2 to 3 slices	fresh gingerroot
handful	fresh raspberries
⅔oz / 2cl	limoncello

AND . . .

chilled wine or cocktail glass

chopping board and sharp knife for ginger

shaker

ice cubes

bar spoon

raspberries and a sprig of mint for garnish

This cocktail was created for Earl Spencer,

brother of the late Diana, Princess of Wales.

He is a regular visitor to the Library Bar.

1

Slice the fresh gingerroot thinly.
Place in the shaker. Muddle with the
end of the bar spoon.

2

Add the raspberries, limoncello, and
vodka. Then add the ice cubes. Shake
sharply so all flavors combine well.
Strain into a chilled glass. Garnish with
two raspberries and a sprig of mint on a
cocktail stick across the glass.

Sweet Sue

INGREDIENTS

1oz / 3cl	cognac
½oz / 1.5cl	Kahlúa
½oz / 1.5cl	frangelica
½oz / 1.5cl	limoncello
½oz / 1.5cl	heavy (double) cream

AND . . .

chilled cocktail or wine glass

mixing glass with ice cubes, and bar spoon

shaker filled with ice cubes

vegetable peeler and semisweet or milk
chocolate slab for garnish

1

Pour the cognac, Kahlúa,
and frangelica into the
mixing glass filled with ice.
Stir quickly. Strain into the
chilled glass.

2

Pour the limoncello and
cream into the shaker. Shake.
Float this creamy mixture
over a bar spoon to create a
layer over the cognac
mixture.

This after-dinner cocktail was made for my patient wife, Sue. It contains all of her favorite ingredients and is perfect for sipping after dinner and late into the night.

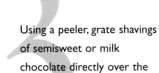

3 Using a peeler, grate shavings of semisweet or milk chocolate directly over the glass onto the creamy layer.

(Champagne) Wonder

INGREDIENTS

2 dashes	Amaretto
	champagne
6	raspberries to purée
⅔oz /2cl	pineapple juice
⅔oz /2cl	orange juice

AND . . .

chilled champagne glass

small bowl and strainer

bar spoon

shaker filled with ice cubes

strawberry for garnish

This was created for the inimitable songwriter and singer

Stevie Wonder during a recent visit to the Library Bar.

1 Make the raspberry pureé by mashing the raspberries with a bar spoon through the strainer over the bowl. Pour the pureé into the shaker.

2 Add the rest of the ingredients, except the champagne, and shake. Strain into the glass and top up slowly with champagne. Make a slit in the bottom of a strawberry and set it on the rim.

When it's midsummer and you feel like throwing a party, a cocktail punch is often the answer to a thirst. In this chapter, each of the three recipes has a unique texture, flavor, and appearance.

You will need a punch bowl or a large pitcher, lots of dry ice cubes, a spirit measure, and lots of fruit for tasty garnishes.

party

punches

Italian Spritzer

INGREDIENTS

3⅓oz / 10cl	Campari
juice of	2 lemons
1 bottle	dry white wine
large bottle	soda water
1 each	small orange, lemon

AND . . .

wine glasses

juicer and large pitcher

dry ice cubes

chopping board and knife for lemon garnish

This punch is refreshing, dry on the palate. Don't add too much fruit in each glass when you serve it. Makes enough for six people.

1

Make the lemon juice. Add it and the other ingredients, except the Campari and soda water, into a pitcher. Add the ice cubes and then the soda water.

2

Add the Campari to give it a pale pink tinge. Stir. Slice one orange and one lemon thinly and add to the pitcher.

Pimm's Cup

INGREDIENTS

1¾oz / 5cl	Pimm's No. 1 Cup
	7 UP or ginger ale
1 each	orange, lemon
	cucumber peel
sprig	fresh small mint leaves

AND . . .

small tumbler

chopping board and sharp knife

large pitcher filled with ice cubes

zester

Pimm's is a gin-based drink that is always drunk with a mixer like 7 UP. This recipe is for one glass. Multiply it by 10 to fill a pitcher.

Make sure each guest has pieces of fruit in his or her glass.

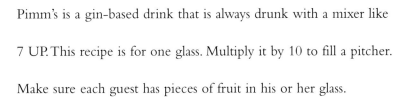

1

Pour the Pimm's into the pitcher filled with ice. Add 7 UP or ginger ale. Add slices of lemon and orange, a few fine strips of cucumber peel, and individual mint leaves. Stir. Add a fresh small sprig of mint as a garnish.

Thanksgiving Punch

INGREDIENTS

1	bottle dry sparkling white wine
3⅓oz / 10cl	brandy
3⅓oz / 10cl	raspberry liqueur
17oz / 50cl	cranberry juice
8⅓oz / 25cl	fresh orange juice
handful	fresh raspberries
handful	cranberries
sprig	fresh mint
2	oranges, sliced

AND . . .

punch bowl and six small tumblers

1 small bag dry ice cubes

small bowl

juicer

chopping board and small knife for slicing oranges

If you don't want to use expensive champagne, use a quality sparkling wine instead. This recipe makes enough for up to six people. Add the ice minutes before guests are due to arrive.

1 Make the fresh orange juice or buy it freshly squeezed. Pour all the ingredients, except the champagne, into a punch bowl. Top up with champagne. Add fruit, berries, and mint.

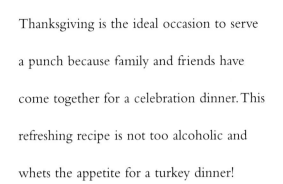

Thanksgiving is the ideal occasion to serve a punch because family and friends have come together for a celebration dinner. This refreshing recipe is not too alcoholic and whets the appetite for a turkey dinner!

2 Add half-slices of both oranges and serve in small tumblers.

nonalcoholic

These are the kinds of cocktails you have when you just don't want a "drink." With the current mood for healthy living, these drinks are perfect palate pleasers. Who would have imagined that exotic fruit juices mixed with the familiar cranberry and orange flavors would create such taste sensations?

temptations

ALL ABOUT COCKTAILS
WITH NO ALCOHOL

The word "nonalcoholic" is enough to signal these cocktails do not contain spirits, liqueurs, or wines. Yet, that does not make them unappealing. When you see them, with ice glistening in the glass, and the garnish sitting sprightly on the glass's rim, you realize just how effective a cocktail they can be at parties where there is pressure to have a "drink."

Basically, these are refreshing drinks made with either dry ice cubes or crushed ice, a combination of juices, fruit, and berries, and even spices. They can be drunk year round and at any event. There is nothing complicated about them, but they do require some thought. The same principles are involved for these cocktails as for alcoholic cocktails. The harmony of individual flavors is essential. As you have learned, too much of one ingredient can completely change the cocktail, so try to follow the ingredients exactly, at least until you are familiar with how the drink should taste. Then feel free to experiment.

I work in the alcohol industry, yet I appreciate that you can create a tasty cocktail without using ingredients that can have an undesired effect. These recipes are great for children and teenagers, especially if you are hosting a large barbecue or evening party. If friends have to drive home, then they are perfect for any time of the day. It's all in the presentation.

Add a chic garnish, such as a red maraschino cherry, or a lemon spiral—the same as you would for an alcoholic cocktail—and the drink immediately becomes a very stylish accessory. Each of these recipes is designed to hold its own against anything alcoholic!

Cranpina

INGREDIENTS

2⅓oz / 7cl	cranberry juice
2⅓oz / 7cl	pink grapefruit juice
2⅓oz / 7cl	pineapple juice
1oz / 3cl	fresh orange juice

AND . . .

highball glass and stirrer

bar spoon

ice cubes

measuring glass for orange juice

chopping board and sharp knife for kiwifruit garnish

1

Fill the highball with ice cubes. Pour the first three ingredients into the glass directly. Stir. Add the orange juice—watch it sink slowly down through the mixture. Cut a slice of kiwifruit and set it on the rim of the glass. Serve with a fancy stirrer.

Ginger Zest

INGREDIENTS

2⅓oz / 7cl	fresh carrot juice
2⅓oz / 7cl	tomato juice
1 teaspoon	honey
juice of	1 lemon
2 to 3 slices	gingerroot
dash	Worcestershire sauce

AND . . .

highball glass

shaker

dry ice cubes

chopping board, sharp knife, and peeler for gingerroot

red cherry tomato, lime, and basil garnish

1 Peel a few large flakes of fresh gingerroot onto a clean chopping board.

2 Place the flakes in a shaker. Muddle to release the ginger's essence, then pour in all remaining ingredients. Add the ice cubes last. Shake well to combine the ginger and juices.

Gingerroot in a cocktail? Yes! It adds a zesty flavor, and it's also good for you, thought to protect your body against unwelcome stomach bugs.

3 Pour into the highball, letting the ice fall into the glass as well. Garnish with half a red cherry tomato, half a slice of lime, and a few basil leaves speared on a cocktail stick.

Lilac Beauty

INGREDIENTS

2 tablespoons low-fat plain yogurt
2⅓oz / 7cl white grape juice
handful fresh blueberries
handful fresh blackberries

AND . . .

tumbler

blender and crushed ice

bar spoon

tea strainer

sprig of mint and blackberry for garnish

1

Combine all the ingredients in a blender until smooth. Add a scoop of crushed ice. Blend quickly again. Strain into a tumbler, pressing with the bar spoon to extract as much flavor as possible. Serve with two berries and a sprig of mint placed on a cocktail stick across the glass.

cocktails for wimps

Pussyfoot

INGREDIENTS

1	free-range egg yolk*
5oz / 15cl	fresh orange juice
1 to 2 dashes	grenadine
juice of	1 lemon
juice of	1 lime

* If you are concerned about eating raw egg yolks, then leave this ingredient out of the recipe.

AND . . .

highball glass filled with ice cubes

shaker filled with ice cubes

small glass and bowl

half-slice of orange and a maraschino cherry for garnish

1

Separate the egg yolk, placing the egg white to one side. (You might want to make an omelet later!) Pour the yolk and juices into a shaker. Shake sharply.

2

Strain into the highball filled with ice cubes. Add 1 to 2 dashes of grenadine. Stir. Garnish with a slice of orange and a maraschino cherry sitting on top of the drink.

Tropicana

INGREDIENTS

½ cup /12cl	coconut milk
2⅓oz /7cl	pineapple juice
2⅓oz /7cl	mango juice
1	small banana, peeled and diced

AND . . .

wine glass or goblet

blender

ice bucket and scoop for crushed ice

chopping board and sharp knife for Cape Gooseberry garnish

1 Place all the ingredients into a blender and blend for a few seconds to pulverize the banana. Add a scoop of crushed ice to the blender. Blend until smooth.

You blend the ingredients before adding any ice to the blender. This makes sure the fruit is mashed into a pulp ready to soak up the juices. This delicious cocktail combines the mild flavors of coconut milk and banana with an exotic hint of mango and pineapple juices.

2 Pour slowly into the glass. Tear carefully down the veins of the Cape Gooseberry to separate the leaves. Pull these back from the orange fruit and arrange the leaves attractively. Cut a slit in the base of the garnish and place it on the rim. Serve!

INDEX

cocktails for wimps

THE MIXOLOGISTS

Fei Xie

Fei, from mainland China, worked there as a television actress. Based in Europe with her family, Fei currently works in the hotel industry. Her ability to smile while shaking some of these delicious cocktails, holding an ice-cold shaker for longer than usual, and obeying the photographer's pleas, was welcome! Fei's favorite cocktail is a classic Bellini—made with fresh white peach juice.

Gillian Kohler

A lawyer from South Africa, Gillian has only recently been introduced to the joy of making cocktails. Now an exponent of muddling berries to capture their freshness, and an advocate of the need to taste every flavor, she will be keeping a watchful eye out when anyone makes her a fruity cocktail in future. Gillian has a passion for Long Island Iced Tea, reminiscent of vacations in Port Elizabeth.

Leo Bryan

He has tasted many fancy cocktails, mainly through his penchant for parties. A DJ from Sydney, Australia, he is also a fan of lager and fine wine. Leo has become expert at blending delicious taste combinations through his recent experience at the photography session. Leo's favorite cocktails are Pina Colada and Pimm's No. 1 Cup.

Camilla Drejer

Camilla, born in Copenhagen, is a political science student and had not mixed a cocktail, despite working in a bar, before the photographic session. A keen skier, she was intrigued by the healthy, fresh, and fruity aspects of the nonalcoholic cocktails. Her favorite cocktail, though, is a classic Sea Breeze.

CREDITS

I would like to thank the staff at The Lanesborough Hotel for their continuing support. Thanks also to my agent, Fiona Lindsay, and to the team at Sterling Publishing Co., Inc. for their commitment to my vision of cocktails for everyone! Lynn Bryan is deeply appreciative of the people at Moet & Chandon for champagne and Hennessy brandy; J. Wray & Nephew (UK) Ltd for Appleton Jamaica Rum; and to First Drinks Brand (UK) for Stolychnaya vodka, Campari, and Glenfiddich whisky.

To James, thanks—great to be in the studio. To all of the talented amateur mixologists, many thanks for making the book such a memorable experience.

Stevan Relic

Stevan, previously owner of a delicatessen, currently works with Salvatore Calabrese. A man mad about Ferrari's racing team, we found his experienced eye and calm manner helpful, and Stevan definitely wins points for making a lime spiral without a zester! The Mojito is his favorite cocktail.

Amanda Hancocks

Amanda had only made cocktails as an amateur prior to this experience. Being a photographer, she had always been on the other side of the camera! Her steady hand was ideal for the layered chapter. Her advice to wimps: "Don't drink before you do it. Unless you need a drink to steady your hand!" Her favorite cocktails include Champagne Cocktail and Cosmopolitan.

Fabrizio Musorella

Other than his passion for shoes, Fabrizio has an Italian passion for cocktails. Titles to his name include Bartender of the Year 2001 and Maker of the Best Classic Cocktail at the 2001 World Cocktail Competition held in Trinidad. He has a wonderful sense of fun, as the photographs reveal. Fabrizio's favorite cocktail is a classic Margarita.